Wandering Verse

An American Keepsake

Elsie Nelson

Wandering Verse, Published June, 2016

Cover Design: Howard Johnson
Interior Design & Layout: Howard Communigrafix, Inc.
Editorial and Proofreading: Eden Rivers Editorial Services; Karen Grennan

 **SDP Publishing**

Published by SDP Publishing, an imprint of SDP Publishing Solutions, LLC.

SDP Publishing
Permissions Department
PO Box 26, East Bridgewater, MA 02333
or email your request to info@SDPPublishing.com.

ISBN-13 (print): 978-0-9968426-0-0
ISBN-13 (ebook): 978-0-9972853-4-5

Library of Congress Control Number: 2016932366

Printed in the United States of America

*This book is dedicated
to the descendants of
Elsie and Ben Nelson.*

Acknowledgments

The brothers and sisters of David Nelson express their appreciation for his devoted efforts in spearheading the publication of this loving tribute to our mom. They also acknowledge the cooperative efforts of all the children of Elsie Nelson, their spouses, and many of Elsie's grandchildren who contributed to the assemblage and publication of this work of art, as did the efforts and encouragement of family friends. Special thank-yous are extended to the following:

- Frederick Nelson provided his computer skills and prodigious efforts to select, edit, and organize our mom's poems for publication;
- Marian Sutton initially ferreted out and preserved handwritten copies of Mom's poems and then supported, counseled, and backed their publication as the sounding board for the family;
- The late Ruth Merrill critically reviewed these poems, discussed them with Mom, provided Mom's perspective, and then helped assemble them;
- The late Kenneth Nelson gave his perspective and faithful support to this publication;
- Dorothy Sarasin created the Foreword and Epilogue and lent her counsel, writing, editing, and organizational skills;
- The late William Nelson provided his dedicated counsel and support;
- Joanne Montague provided the perspective of a younger member of the family and faithfully supported, helped to organize, and encouraged this publication;
- Roger M. Junak, a friend of the family, painted the watercolor of the Nelson farm that appears on the cover and consented to its use;
- Richard T. Carne, Mom's artistically talented nephew, over the years furnished his artwork to the family and authorized the use of his illustrations;
- Lisa Akoury-Ross of SDP Publishing Solutions provided her publishing expertise and professional guidance throughout this process;
- Lisa Schleipfer of Eden Rivers Editorial Services edited and organized the manuscript for publication;
- Howard Johnson at Howard Communigrafix, Inc. offered his fantastic creative talent to the layout and design of the book; and
- Kim Kortes, David's legal secretary, patiently lent her computer skills to the project, prepared the manuscript for submission to SDP Publishing Solutions, and encouraged its publication.

Foreword

Elsie Nelson, née Elsie Carne, was born in Ishpeming, Michigan on September 28, 1906 to English immigrants from Cornwall, England. She, her sister, and three brothers grew up under the loving hand of their mother. The family was stable—albeit poor—throughout her childhood. Early on as a child she possessed an inner strength to go forward, even on legs wizened with rickets, and oftentimes walked miles to deliver her father's lunch.

Elsie was an above average student who excelled in English and American Literature. Whitman, Emerson, and Thoreau became her inspirations and she reveled in their poems and essays.

On March 1, 1924, Elsie entered into a marriage that would last for 61 years and produce eight children. Her beloved husband, Ben Nelson, died on Good Friday, April 6, 1985.

Nothing in her childhood could have prepared her for the Great Depression of the 1930s. Raising their family in a hand-hewn log house, without employment or money, the couple endured one of the cruelest tests of human endurance. Ironically, in a land of vast iron ore resources, each day became a test of survival and hope that waxed and waned with the moon. Her family gratefully acknowledges her fortitude and this forbearing verse:

> *We have no other mandate*
> *But to do the things we must;*
> *Go with the tide at its lowest ebb,*
> *Hang on tight and trust.*

This timeless collection of verse, written exclusively by Elsie Nelson over a period of six decades, provides a significant degree of naturalism and humanity. From her isolated rural environment she reflected her thoughts through verse. It could be said that her pen was her voice, her freedom, and her friend.

Dorothy Sarasin

---

[1]Further insight into the circumstances surrounding Elsie's life and times can be found in a memoir entitled *River of Iron* by David Lee, Xlibris LLC 2014.

Elsie Nelson (1974)

Fragments of thought are exhibited here,
Ideas upon which to ponder.
If the verse seems a wee bit strange,
'Tis that thought is so prone to wander.

ECN

Table of Contents

Chapter 1 **Home**

Home Is the Heart 2
Bootstraps 3
The Aging Farm 4
The Front Porch 5
Old Things Are Treasures 6
The Old Wood Stove 7
Mother's Pantry 8
Mother's Bread 9
The Forsaken House 10
Togetherness 11
Lamplight 12

Chapter 2 **All Creatures Great and Small**

Home 14
A Wonderful Friend 15
Fall of a Giant 16
Neighbors 17
The Butterfly 18
To a Dead Woodchuck 18
Stray Kitten 19
Unshackled Swallow 20
To a Woodthrush 20
Company 21
The Window Box 22
Little Chipmunk 23
His Majesty, the Crow 24
Simplicity 25

Chapter 3 **Personal Reflections**

Thinking 28
Writing 29
Over My Shoulder 30
Reflections 31
Reclusivity 32
Ambition 33

The Great Redeemer 34
A Place to Be Me 35
Me 36
Time for Reflection 37
Reminiscing 38
Courage 38
Solitude 39
Perspective 40
Writer's Cramp 41
Wishing 42

Chapter 4   **A Time For All Seasons**

Look to the Sunrise 44
January.. 45
The Blizzard of '82 46
Not for Me 47
Spring 48
Springtime.. 49
Springtime to Me 50
A Late Storm.. 51
Variations... 52
Sunshine 53
Ode to Summer 54
Stardust 54
Contentment 55
Autumn... 55

Chapter 5   **The Human Spirit**

Meandering... 58
Look Up 59
As You Look at It.. 60
In His Presence 61
Life 62
A Sonnet to Faith 63
Vision 64
Serenity 65
Gratification.. 66
Resurrection... 67
Time Heals All.. 68

Echoes 69
Wisdom 70
Helmsman 70
Abstraction 71
The Nucleus... 72
Not Forgotten... 73

Chapter 6 **Children**

Shoelaces.. 76
Little Dirty Faces 77
A Matter of Opinion... 78
The Resting Hour 79
All Bugs Take Care!.. 80
Boy of Four 81
Youth.. 82
The Windblown Lass 83
I Want Mommy 84
Graduation 85

Chapter 7 **It's a Living**

Mamma's Wisdom.. 88
Go Walkin' 89
Day by Day 90
Eating Time 91
The Local Train... 92
Priorities 93
The Weekly Wash 94
A Day Off... 95
Pondering 96
Holidays 97
Day's End.. 98
Work... 99
The Old Quartet 100
Untitled 100

Chapter 8 **Voices of Others**

Old Friends Are the Best.. 102
The Weekly Bias 103
Faces.. 104

A Matter of Years 105
Gossip.. 106
Faces from My Youth..107
A Master of Opinion 108
A Disagreement.. 109
Lady of Gloom 110
A Secret...111

Chapter 9 **The Golden Years**

My Mother 114
Grandma 115
Relaxation 116
Grandma's Apron..117
Grandma's Day..117
Grandpa's Knee...118
Grandpa's Teacup..119
Grandpa's Slippers... 120
Seniority... 121
Destiny.. 122
The Carver 123
Sonnet to Getting Old.. 124
Senility 125
Being Old 126
The Oneness of Time 127

Chapter 10 **Sense and Nonsense**

End of the Line... 130
How You View It 131
A Big Deal.. 132
Naturally... 133
Obedience 133
A Discussion... 134
Untitled 135
Untitled 136

Epilogue

Epilogue... 137

**In addition to the poems listed here, selected untitled quatrains and poems created by Elsie Nelson have been interspersed in the chapters. These poems will be distinguished in a different font.

Introduction

Here in a rambling moment
Expressed in language terse,
Is a gleaning of thought from yesterday's page
Revealing itself in verse.

ECN

CHAPTER

1

Home

I used to long for laborless days

At a time when life seemed perverse,

But now I think the bread was sweeter

When I had to bake it first.

ℰC𝓃

Home Is the Heart

It takes but little to make a home
When love is at its core,
Curtains bright and glowing lamps
And a welcome at the door.

Friendly, smiling faces
And warmth most everywhere,
It takes so little to make a home
When the folks within it care.

No matter how grand the dwelling,
Or how tasteful is the mold,
It may not be satisfactory,
If the atmosphere is cold.

Bootstraps

Raising a troop of children
Was a fine way to pass the years.
We were too busy for thoughts of self,
No time for tears.

We enjoyed games and picnics together.
Sundays were for rest.
When a child was overwhelmed by woes,
We did whatever was best.

Toil and trouble and restless feet,
They grew and grew.
We know at last the deep satisfaction
of having raised a crew.

The Aging Farm

I've come home at last to the aging farm
Where as a child I roamed.
Though time has altered this much-loved place,
It is still my favorite home.

Gone is the silvered planking barn
And the little, red water shed.
Gone is the mill and the old horse stable
That sheltered our Bonny and Ned.

The cottage shingles are faded with age
As it nestles against the hill,
As though fearing the blast of wintry cold
That billows about it still.

Though all has changed in the passing of years,
Hard hit by time and weather,
Nothing can change the love in our hearts
Nor our joy at gathering together.

The Front Porch

When I was a child, homes had a veranda
Where one rested from daily chores;
Folks rocked and talked on warm summer evenings
'Til dusk sent them scampering indoors.

Recipes and latest in fashion
Were oft shouted along the street;
At times the exuberant crickets crooned along
From their under-porch retreat.

Folks seemed much more neighborly then,
When concern for others was oft a passion;
I think one of life's simple pleasures departed
When the front porch went out of fashion.

Old Things Are Treasures

There's a faded old couch in the corner,
Its brocade of roses worn;
There are those who say, "It must be replaced,
It no longer serves to adorn."

But the decrepit old couch has a place in my heart,
It is more than a place to recline.
It is part of the years I have lived in this house,
I, too, have changed with time.

When I grow weary of worldly things,
And no longer wish to roam,
I lay my head on the faded old couch,
And know that at last I'm home.

The Old Wood Stove

The old iron stove in the kitchen,
When I was a child of eight,
Had a warming closet and a singing kettle,
And, oh, the wood it ate!

To fill the usually empty wood box
Was a never-ending chore,
But the reward of a cozy, warming fire
Was worth it all and more.

The wood fire soothed our wintry hearts;
It boiled water for a toddy;
It baked and cooked and stewed our meals—
A mute servant to everybody.

Of the many memories of childhood,
None seem more real or profound
Than my recollection of the old wood stove—
With loved ones gathered 'round.

Shoes lined up beneath a bench—
Papa, sister, brother—
Inform folks who come to visit
That inside is a busy mother.

Mother's Pantry

Mother's pantry long ago
Was a wondrous sight to see,
With rows and rows of preserves and such
Displayed attractively.
There were peppermints and licorice sticks
And jars of every hue,
Holding secret ingredients
That only mother knew.
Pastry boards with pies and cakes,
And many little dishes
Filled with cookery so numerous,
Even the smell was delicious.
Today few folks have a Mother's Pantry,
And, though we have cupboards galore,
We'd be at a loss to operate
If it weren't for the market store.

Mother spends many hours
Cleaning up the place.
At night she's too spent to take a bath
Or wash her tired face.

Mother's Bread

When I think upon my childhood days
What first comes to my head,
And fills me with nostalgia,
Is when Mother baked her bread.

Each week she baked six golden loaves,
Aromatic and delectably done.
Mother's face hovered over all,
Pink and pretty as a bride in June.

The smell that filled the kitchen
Left us drooling and awaiting,
And we fussed and coaxed to receive the crust
From Mother's weekly baking.

Mother works from early morn
Cleaning all that has a name.
Yet, when we go to bed at night,
Everything looks the same.

The Forsaken House

There's a house on a hill at the end of our street
Enclosed by a wrought-iron fence.
It is sprawling, old, and decrepit,
Towered, gabled, and immense.

It is sheltered by evergreens growing tall,
And nearby is a moss-covered well.
I'm quite sure if the house could speak to me
It would have wonderful stories to tell.

There would, undoubtedly, have been romance;
Times both of laughter and despair.
Birth and death and broken hearts
All could have happened there.

But time changes all, and the house stands mute,
A lovely symbol of a by-gone way,
When others laughed and loved and cried
The same as we do today.

Dwell in a lone secluded place
With endless forest, little more;
Be a recluse if you must,
But place a welcome by the door.

Togetherness

In wintry weather our old house
Breathes and echoes from end to end.
It speaks to us of daily living
In tones we comprehend.

Refrigerator hums consistently,
Mr. Furnace roars along,
House trembles and creaks in accompaniment
'Til the rafters echo the song.

There's a moaning and groaning in the
chimney place
When storms and gales abound.
The ridge pole creaks and the windows rattle
In a cacophony of sound.

But on a slumberous summer evening
When night's shadows come a-creeping,
All that prevails is a muffled hum.
Tread softly!! House is sleeping!

Lamplight

A lamp is such a comforting thing,
Diffusing warmth throughout the place,
Imparting a halo of glowing light
To each expectant face.

A mother is the lamp that lights the family,
The glow that keeps all together;
And when a good mother passes away
The light goes out forever.

Nothing ceases because you are low,
All hums and rattles; the winds still blow;
The evening paper is flung at your door;
All proceeds as it has before.

If days are long and lonely,
And the sky has lost its blue,
If you feel a bit concerned,
Happiness may be up to you.

CHAPTER

2

All Creatures Great and Small

Flowers of a varied hue and sort
Bloom across the continent.
So plentiful are these works of art
We overlook the accomplishment.

CR

Home

Oh, let me dwell content where the magnificent pine
Rises heavenward from earthy clod.

Let me feel the dry crunch of copper needles
Beneath me on the rustling sod.

Let me hear the chant and the playful whistle
Of the wind in the swaying boughs,

And the melodious tones of exuberant thrush
Professing his love with eternal vows.

Let me hear the ripple of a nearby brook
As it rushes headlong toward the sea,

And I shall know all I need of nature's way
And of quiet contentment revealed in empathy.

A Wonderful Friend

You're not much of a dog, I'll admit.
Your coat isn't shiny nor sleek,
And you'd rather just set than be a setter,
Any old day in the week.

Through the summer days we traveled together,
Through field and countryside.
With tongue drooling out, you were there, little pal,
Running along by my side.

But summer must end, and I had to leave.
And you stood on the trail and whined.
When I said "Home, boy," you slunk away,
Your tail drooping low behind.

I'll be back again, boy, when duty is o'er
With footsteps no longer lagging.
What I want to see first is you, good old pal,
With your tail in the air and wagging.

A man who owns a beagle dog,
And thinks his pet is great,
Makes one sort of envious
When he throws his dog a steak.

Fall of a Giant

A pine tree once grew quite near my window
With great branches sweeping out,
Providing shade and comfort, too,
For little creatures 'round about.

How often I basked in its loveliness
And listened to the wind's sad song,
But the beautiful tree meant little to me
'Til suddenly one day it was gone.

Two woodsmen came and felled the tree.
To them it was board feet of wood,
But I shall not forget the lonely place
Where once a giant stood.

Neighbors

Ants are such strange little creatures,
To observe them is such a delight;
One wonders what spirit moves them
To work without end day and night.

They are so very prodigious,
Communistic, energetic, and sure.
Though their choice of abode is absurd,
The young always seem to mature.

Then, busy as their forebears,
They commence with much aplomb.
Heaping sand one grain at a time
For the new little ants to come.

If you are ever in doubt where to find one,
Although there are ways galore,
Just follow the hills near the walkway—
They lead right up to my door.

The Butterfly

When I observe some of God's creatures
I sometimes feel second rate.
I'm sure I could learn from a butterfly
If it could but communicate.

To a Dead Woodchuck

Sleek of coat, and quick of eye,
You burrowed beneath the wall,
And had no way of knowing
Of your unmitigated gall.

Poor little creature, I found in you
A persistence much like me;
A strong desire, an urgent need,
To house your family.

But a man's home is his very own,
And a wall must be firm and lasting.
So poor, intrepid chuck you had to go,
And I'm left with a tear at your passing.

Stray Kitten

Are you lost little kitten?
Have you strayed from home?
Or are you no longer wanted,
And left quite free to roam?

You've quite a charming aspect
With your cute bewhiskered face,
And blue eyes sort of pleading
For a warm and friendly place.

Come with me and share my lodging,
For I'm a wee bit lonely, too.
You'd find in me a companion
Doubtless as pleased as you.

For companions must be compatible,
Be they man or beast,
And if the love is mutual,
Kind matters not the least.

Our cat is fond of napping,
And lounges in an easy chair.
He considers the chair his headquarters,
And will not allow you there.

Unshackled Swallow

With wings outspread he soars aloft,
A tiny blur against the sky.
A lesson in tenacity,
For a mortal such as I.

So frail, so minute, so vulnerable,
In a vast and airy sea.
Yet, I who watch must envy him
His boundless liberty.

To a Woodthrush

Oh matriarch of songsters,
Oh builder of nestlings' abode,
Little architect of the woodland,
Unheedful of style or mode:
What spirit moves thy feathered breast?
What prompts your roun-de-lay?
Is it borne on the wind in mysterious whispers?
Or does a pilot show the way?

Company

I stalk the forest in solitude
In a silence so profound,
Even the rustling of the leaves
Seems to profane hallowed ground.

I am not dismayed, however,
For here and there a creature lurks,
And I am not surprised at all
When suddenly a cricket chirps.

We humans fuss and fret over trifles,
Concerned with desires of all sorts and kinds.
The diligent birds take life as it comes
And never seem to mind.

The Window Box

My neighbor has a window box
Of geraniums red and white.
When breezes caress the tender blooms,
They sway and nod with delight.

Passersby with happy visage
Express pleasure and admiration,
And those confined within the household
Find joy in contemplation.

Winged creatures hover o'er
With fluttering, pulsating wings,
And sometimes a robin comes calling
And opens his throat to sing.

Little Chipmunk

Beneath a widespread cherry tree
He gathers his winter's lode,
Then scolds and tells me emphatically
I'm trespassing on his abode.

Little fellow, have no fear,
Your store is safe from me.
I've no desire to encroach upon
Your right of tenancy.

For heaven's sun gleams down alike
On creatures here beneath.
I, no more, in my roofed domain
Than you, little guy, 'neath a leaf.

Little porcupine on my stairway
Considering it your right.
I'll not proceed to my domain;
I'll not promote a fight.

His Majesty, the Crow

Black and shiny and seldom alone
He perches atop a barren tree.
His sharp, beady eyes miss nothing—
Oh no, sir, not even me.

His presence is known in a raucous way,
His piercing call heard from afar;
Soon a cacophony of calls respond,
Each contributor black as tar.

Forgive his often haughty ways,
Do not envy his ebony wing,
For proud as he I marvel and see
His majesty, who is King.

Take the cheer out of happiness,
The blue out of the sky,
Take the birds that sing when on the wing,
And life is but a sigh.

Simplicity

No need to travel the world around
For the lovely and sublime,
For the finest gem or work of art
May lose its charm with time.

I'd much rather look about me,
For when all is said and done,
Heaven's glory may reflect from a dewy flower
Or from a pine tree glistening in the sun.

When skies are azure,
And clouds are tinted gold,
A woodland bathed in sunlight
Is a glorious sight to behold.

3

Personal Reflections

We have no other mandate
But to do the things we must.
Go with the tide at its lowest ebb,
Hang on tight and trust.

PCN

Thinking

I'm sort of a small world figure;
I dislike to leave the nest.
I would change the way of those in sorrow,
If I knew what things were best.

I'd feed the hungry and lift the spirits
Of those beings very sad,
And try to change the wayward ones
From ways that make them bad.

I'd love each broken-hearted child,
And appreciate the good.
If only I were great enough,
To do the things I would.

The story of my life
Would make astounding fiction.
When I speak very honestly,
It seems like contradiction.

Writing

If I could write and write,
From here to eternity,
I don't believe I could tell enough
About the myriad things I see.

———⟨⟨⟨∞⟩⟩⟩———

*The mind should be a receptacle
With portals opened wide;
So that whatever beauty of thought prevails
May find its way inside.*

Over My Shoulder

I have reached life's sunset hour,
And all that has passed and gone
Parades before me in a solemn procession
Of memories profound.

I hear again the lonely call
Of a hoot owl in the night,
And feel again the crawling dread
That such things oft excite.

I remember the pure and penetrating anthem
Of vespered church bells ringing,
And the sudden flutter of nesting swallows
Uprooted into winging.

I know a place where the trembling wildlife
From tree and bower is heard,
While the brisk running stream 'neath the rusted bridge
Flows onward unperturbed.

Mistakes are a part of the living process,
No matter how we try,
One must go on and attempt to accept them.
All passes by.

Reflections

In the daylight hours
I dash with spirit high
With never a pause for quiet—
Nor even a tired sigh.

Friends I greet quite amiably;
We laugh and I serve tea.
I drive the children home from school,
Happily hearing their shouts of glee.

But at evening with the household still,
When twilight steals my mood,
I find my happiest moment
In quiet solitude.

*I don't worry about syntax,
Or if what I say is properly said.
I write what I know of living,
There's not much else in my head.*

Reclusivity

Too late to be a heroine,
If ever I really could.
Too late to regret an occasional rebellion,
Even if I would.

But not too late for impish moods
That come from time to time.
I can be whatever I want
In the inner recesses of my mind.

Fortunately, even in my mind,
I sustain a bit of shock.
I'm very glad that no one dreams
What occurs to me in thought.

You can run away from duty;
You can run away; it's true.
But no matter what your troubles may be,
You cannot run away from you.

Ambition

Isn't it grand what nerve can do
When you no longer have it to boast.
I'd climb to the highest of cliffs; doggone,
With the ease of a mountain goat.

I'd clean up every nook and cranny
Most any time, and never swerve,
And do a "zillion" other things
If I only had the nerve.

*Wisdom is a virtue,
It helps to keep one sane,
But greater yet is courage,
When one is in pain.*

The Great Redeemer

How comforting is the thought of sleep,
A boon to all mankind.
Sleep is to the weary a welcome respite,
Sleep is balm to a tired mind.

The fretful child finds solace in slumber,
The anxious forget their woes.
Much pain and hurt is eased away
In sleep's curative repose.

When overwhelmed with cares of the day,
Too weary to think or plan,
What a blessing to find a quiet place
And drift off into slumberland.

The hurts in life are paramount,
The good is lost in shade,
Yet, when you take inventory,
Your sorrow is certain to fade.

A Place to Be Me

'Tis not the thing, I'm often told,
To be different than the throng.
Whatever is thought acceptable,
You do, or you don't belong.

And so I wrap my wayward self
And put me quite away.
To be one's self in a patterned world,
One must await a solitary day.

I arise in the morning,
A frisky pup.
Back to bed,
No one's up.

Me

When I'm down and feeling low,
Perhaps about two feet tall,
I think how nice to hop a plane
And drift away from it all.

But I know that though I travel far,
Even across the sea,
Right along with the baggage and all
Will be little old pesky me.

When you are a bit weary,
Nothing is as you would,
Forget about the negatives—
Take time to count the good.

When the vicissitudes of life
Overwhelm you and you cannot cry,
You attempt to be unaware of hurt,
And wonder why.

Time for Reflection

They speak of solitude as lonely time,
Which can be true, I quite agree,
But there are times when a moment alone
Is more desired than a symphony.

A time to reflect in the stillness,
Away from the world's mad stirring,
To hear again the tick of a laboring clock
And a sleeping cat's soft purring.

Count your blessings when you're sad.
Count to ten; do not get mad.
Count the friends whose love you sought.
Love cannot be bartered, lent, or bought.

Reminiscing

They came for the weekend
My daughter and spouse.
We conversed for many an hour.
They have gone, the house is silent.
I sit beside the only reminder—
A silver vase with a lovely flower.

Courage

No day is so perfect
That it has no hurt to tell.
But with peace within
And the courage to win,
We often do quite well.

Solitude

A country house with shutters green,
At the end of a rugged drive,
Seems to be too solitary,
To harbor folks inside.

Almost hidden by birch and pine,
It nestles beneath boughs reaching.
'Tis a comforting refuge,
When life's worries are defeating.

Place your tired feet on an ottoman;
Reflect beside a glowing flame.
Forget the cares of yesterday,
And begin your life again.

My entire day seemed to be all wrong;
I was sad as I could be,
Until I came to realize
The trouble was really me.

Perspective

We are prone to grumble,
When it's hot, we long for cold.
We look at folks no longer humble,
As hoarding heaps of gold.

The rich long for days of work,
The laborer longs for rest.
A wizard would have trouble explaining,
What outcome is the best.

Take life with a grain of salt,
And with a certain aplomb.
No matter how you view it,
You must accept whatever comes.

How often we lubricate the air
With rounds of pious chatter;
Yet when the simple truth abides
Goodness, kindness, and faith are what really matter.

I'm not a perfect saint;
I'm not even trying.
If I professed to be one,
I'd be lying.

Writer's Cramp

I love to write and hold a pen,
It seems to challenge me.
Though nothing that I dream of,
May make history.

Yet, I can tell of the outspreading tree,
With branches that bow when I pass,
Of a life devoted to duty,
And a certain amount of class.

Life's errors, fraught with hurt
And despairing stings,
Are merely pain-laden stepping stones
To better things.

Wishing

I would that I had been wiser
In the early time of life;
Perhaps I'd have been a perfect mom,
Without one thought of strife.

And if there had been elves
To do the worst of chores,
I would have found occasion
To indulge the out-of-doors.

Yet, knowing I had the vision
To be a good man's wife,
I now look upon the days that passed,
As the best days of my life.

Life has been a bit of a challenge;
Don't ask me how.
I'd have waited for better days,
If I knew what I know now.

Coo a little, learn a little
Work 'til setting sun.
Love and laugh and cry a little
Before the race is won.

CHAPTER

4

A Time For All Seasons

Winter is sometimes grey and dreary;

Birds warble no more from leafy boughs.

But just when I'm feeling sorriest,

I find a ray of sunshine

Peek-a-booing through the clouds.

ℰℂ𝓃

Look to the Sunrise

All seasons have their glorious moments
And days of sheer delight—
When sunlight bathes our world by day,
And starlight graces night.

However grand the day, I look to morning
Before dawn's bold rise to power,
When shadowy, mute, and majestically serene
Day has her finest hour.

*Unfathomable is the wee little star
That glitters in a measureless sky.
Yet seeming of more significance
Than the mere speck of dust that is I.*

January

When winter chills you to the bone,
And causes shakes and shivers;
When wind's fury in the chimney place
Tells a tale of cold and blizzards;
When you would rather be indoors
With a book you've read before;
It will even be cold when the sun appears.
That is January's décor.

Looking out at ice and snow,
Barren trees with limbs bent low,
Frost upon the window pane;
Winter has arrived again.

If snow was green and trees were blue,
I'm sure we'd fill with fright,
And immediately want to change
Winter back to white.

The Blizzard of '82

A capricious sun peeked cautiously
From skies of greyish hue,
As if to sort of compensate
For the absent skies of blue.

But even the sun's ebullience
Could not ease the bitter chill,
Nor lessen the wind's aggressive roar
As it carved images on the hill.

Deserted streets were everywhere
As if all had a wintry vacation;
Most folks preferring the indoor warmth
To the strong wind's penetration.

How patiently those pent folks listened
For an end to the wild wind's blasts;
Knowing that after it had its fling
That soon it, too, would pass.

Yesterday was cool but gorgeous,
Windblown and golden hued.
Today winter's snow is on every post,
I consider nature very rude.

Not for Me

When wintry blasts are bitter cold
And gusty winds abound,
Filling the house and chimney place
With many an eerie sound,

I sit upon my window seat
And peer out moodily;
The scene, though quite majestic,
Holds no special charm for me.

Winter is for the young in years,
And the young must have their fling,
But it seems that even the brooding hills,
Mute and silent, wait for spring.

Spring drips from the rooftop,
Sun makes everything bright.
Winter must be notified,
It's time to say goodnight.

Spring

Have you heard the river's babbled tune
As it rushes to the sea?

Have you heard the wind's soft lullaby
As it shakes the apple tree?

Have you listened to the caroling birds
As they nestle in the sun?

Have you seen the lengthening shadows
When the day's symphony is done?

Have you heard a new and joyous note
When the little children sing?

Then I guess I don't have to tell you;
I'm sure you know it's spring.

Springtime

Each day I lounge on a divan,
Looking out on pine-studded hills.
The wind in the trees,
The sounds of the breeze,
Create a desire to be very still.

For a time I forget the hustle
And bustle of chores being done;
I know the joy of spring returning.
Soon I will see a fluttering bee,
And apple blossoms gleaming in the sun.

*Green fields and dandelions,
And windblown daisies nodding;
Piney hills and buzzing bees,
And workmen homeward plodding.*

Springtime to Me

Right in the middle of glorious spring,
When the whole world seems in rhyme,
We women have to spoil it all
By what is known as cleaning time.

Things get aired and washed and scrubbed.
The smell of paint is in the air.
Curtains come down and put in the tub,
No relaxation anywhere.

But when this madness passes,
And we resume our normal routine,
How wonderfully satisfying it is
To have things sparkling clean.

A Late Storm

Winter's fury had passed, it seemed.
March wind and rain prevailed.
The snow had succumbed to the warmth of spring,
And e're long summer would be hailed.

But spring is a bit unpredictable,
And no sooner had we welcomed her wiles,
When along came another bleak snowstorm
To keep us indoors for a while.
Soon I will see a fluttering bee,
And apple blossoms gleaming in the sun.

Some folks like to stay indoors
When rain is dribbling down,
But it's nice to don slicker and galoshes
And slosh all over town.

Variations

Today is mild and airy,
A day to truly enjoy.
Changeable weather in spring
Can at times annoy.

But beyond the clouds and changing sky,
We find a fresh new start,
Sunny days and refreshing rain,
And hope within the heart.

Sunshine

Dark and cloud-infested sky
All around I see,
Promise naught but bone chilling rains,
Which drip from rooftop and tree.

Sunless days and wind-whipped nights,
Oft sleepless, too, and bleak,
And those who wait for spring's denouement,
Find no solace in the drip and creak.

Spring is a capricious time of year,
And just when you're feeling most glum,
A ray of sunlight brightens the day,
And "Howdy do!" says the saucy old sun.

Roses are in bloom.
The sky is blue.
I'm indoors
Enjoying the view.

Ode to Summer

Summer is an industrious bee,
Or a hummingbird whirling in ecstasy,
Hovering above gay perfumed flowers
Heart attuned to the fleeting hours.

Summer is a rose and a rushing stream,
'Tis a bald-faced eagle's piercing scream,
'Tis a sunny beach and golden sand,
Or a street parade and a marching band.

Stardust

A picture window on a starlit summer night
Is a thing of sheer delight.
Though no astronomers are we,
We glory in the sight.

Each ordered star, like a well-placed lamp,
Combines with moonglow to light the skies,
Illuminating the face of an awed little child
With wonder in his eyes.

Contentment

I love to be abed at night
When the rain comes drizzling down.
The pit-a-pat upon the roof
Has such a cozy sound.

I huddle in my quilted robe
And watch the drooling dollops,
As they tumble down the window glass
In bubbly little drops.

Each tiny rivulet plays a tune
Upon my windowpane.
How very nice to be secure
A'listening to the rain.

Autumn

The bright-red roses have faded now.
The heavily scented lilacs have long gone.
Summer's bloom and balmy air
Delights and invigorates and passes on.

Denouement of summer brings autumnal breezes
And colored scenery brilliant and gay.
'Tis nature's way of announcing flagrantly
That winter will soon be on the way.

5

The Human Spirit

Lifting chalice, holding dew
So sweet and full of grace.
I look into a blossom's heart
And see the Maker's face.

CN

Meandering

The mind is often a traveler
Wandering far and wide.
Like a meandering river—
Drifting aimlessly with the tide.

And so, my mind, I've let you free
To ramble where you will,
Wandering into nooks and crannies
Meandering over the hill.

I'm not really a shining sort
Nor even righteous and good,
I go my way, and try each day,
To do the things I should.

Look Up

Eyes downcast on life's grim journey,
Burdened with worldly care,
Modern man travels a rough-hewn highway
Oft tasting of hurt and despair.

Man, lift up your eyes to the dark pine hills,
See the gold gleaming sun on its ordered way.
Listen and wonder at the fluted thrush,
As he carols his sweet exuberant lay.

Little has changed since time's beginning
In this magnificent cosmic sea;
Take time from habit to view the stars
And know a lesson in constancy.

Minute lanterns light night's infinite way;
Hung there by Hands unseen.
A canopy of gems embraces man;
He looks to the heavens and so leaves the mean.

As You Look at It

They say that the earth was formed of gases
Once blown away from the sun,
And all we are, and seem to be,
Is of such phenomenon.

Then who created the umbrageous oak
From a tiny acorn seed?
Or made water to flow in sparkling streams
Upon which the seedlings feed?

What miracle gas creates a child
To grow to be a man,
With eyes to see a twinkling star
And ears to hear a band?

Who made each creature a certain kind,
A fish, a bird, a beast?
Who made a rose exquisite,
Or an orange for a feast?

Each day I find new miracles
That keep me ever learning,
And the only gas that seems apparent
Comes from the lips of the undiscerning.

In His Presence

When I was a child,
I attended church,
Though not of an age to care.

When I grew up,
I searched for God,
And found Him everywhere.

If you doubt a master plan
When all about you flaunts His hand,
Plant a seed almost too minute to see
And know that a miracle will produce a tree.

Life

Life is a base for varied events,
Strung across the years,
Stuffed with elements of good and bad,
Often bringing tears.

Live with faith, go forward with courage,
Forget the stabs and stings.
Make each and every vicissitude
A base for better things.

A Sonnet to Faith

He breathes in the dark pine's whispered lay,
In the soft-lapping ocean's white-foamed spray,
In the ancient sunset's glorious view,
And the soft-twirled rose's brilliant hue.

His presence emanates from each leaf-trimmed tree,
Radiantly showing His strength and majesty.

See the stars in their ordered place;
Observe sweetness and trust in a child's face;
Gaze on mountains full of grace.

Let those who doubt the Creator's care
Look about and find Him everywhere.

Vision

Life is an opaque obstacle course
Where we amateurs stumble and stray;
We know the stretch and the hazards,
But no lantern lights the way.

Lord, give us intellect to know thy will
That we may open life's doors with an unerring key,
And having clear vision to set our sails
Come unsullied home to thee.

What power made a cherry tree,
Or a living from the sod?
Plant a seed and nurture it,
But don't forget who is God.

Serenity

Not in the whirl of human events,
Not in pompous society,
Not in the stream of shopping crowds,
Can one find serenity.

Give me the illuminating stars at night,
Or a tree-lined path to trudge,
Or let me rest by a stream with a book,
And a king could not get me to budge.

Gratification

To grumble is a human trait,
Crying out for the things we desire,
Oft overlooking the good and our blessings,
We take for granted what we ought to admire.

How sad it must be to know of hunger
With not a soul to care,
Or to live in filth and ignorance
And no compassion for our despair.

Think how sweet the salubrious air
On a breezy summer day;
How fortunate to walk in freedom
Enjoying all along the way.

So much good fortune comes our way
In this superbly run estate;
No desired thing has such priority
That grateful folks can't wait.

Resurrection

Fate with sudden ferocity
May arrest the sparrow in flight,
And toss him broken and bruised to the ground
With swift and terrible might.

Man may be plunged from his estate,
Robbed of the fruits of travail,
As the maple is quickly denuded
In the lightning twist of the gale.

May small men, jesting, combine with fate
To twist and grind him low,
'Til broken his wings and groveling,
He lies in the scum below.

Yet there in the mire,
The muck and the mold,
Pulsates, undefiled,
His invincible soul.

Time Heals All

Our daily lives hold much of hurt,
Hard put to keep from crying.
Valiant must we ever be
To keep from hopeless sighing.

While the martyred ones hold back their tears,
And the brave give no quarter to sorrow,
The trusting wipe their dewy eyes
Knowing all will be well tomorrow.

Don't waste your time in anxieties—
A futile cause at best.
Keep heart and mind in faithful goodness
And God will do the rest.

Echoes

When the pains of fate's inordinate stabs
Offend and dismay to unbearable degree,
Tears of frustration pervade the soul, and
There's an intense desire to fight or flee.

In frustration and anger, one heaves and sighs
With complete abhorrence of things adverse,
Unaware that banging one's head on relentless stone
Is of no consequence, save for the hurts.

Be patient and forbearing.
Have faith when hope is gone.
If you listen very carefully,
You will hear an angel song.

Wisdom

A curious child with questing eyes
Asked me a question,
Much to my surprise.
"If I were to seek the trait in life
Most desirable to me,
What would it be?"

I pondered, then said "Wisdom."
"Wisdom to live from day to day.
Wisdom to keep thy feet from straying
From thy Maker's way."

Helmsman

When loneliness comes upon us,
We choose a solitary nook,
Attempting to find solutions,
Not contained in any book.

Softly the breezes blow,
Entering our quiet little realm.
They tell us to look beyond,
To the One who holds the helm.

Abstraction

The lush pines that envelop me
Whisper sonnets they alone know.
Alone, transfixed, on a parapet of green,
I am engrossed in their mystic glow.

It doesn't cost the smallest dime
To be happy and content.
Have a mind to absorb what is there,
Do not seek a world of multitudinous events.

But one filled with moments,
And someone there;
Joyous moments,
And some folks who care.

The Nucleus

Love is often a surprising thing;
It is oft very hard to obtain.
Yet, it comes quite unexpectedly,
Like a sudden shower of rain.
It may be remembered as love for one's mate,
For a mother long since gone,
Or for a child with a gentle voice
Who sings a tender song.
When at times we note it's worth,
We stop a moment to pray,
"Let me be like a dear child,
If only one hour a day."

Not Forgotten

Darling, you've departed,
Somehow I stumbled through;
Knowing from my childhood
I must do what I have to do.

I'm not hurting, really;
I have folks who care.
I still lie about when weary,
In your comforting easy chair.

I like to think you're waiting,
With blue eyes aglow;
When at last I'm with you again,
'Tis all I have to know.

CHAPTER

6

Children

Beat the drums for the rich and famous,

Shout praises as the renowned pass by.

But keep a watch for little children

Lost in this world of passersby.

ECN

Shoelaces

Seated on soft grey carpeting,
Little boy of four.
Clutching laces to lace his shoes
As Mommy had done before.

"I'm a big boy now, Mommy,
I can lace my own,"
And he struggled with the laces
To show Mommy how it was done.

But somehow the pointed laces
Seemed to miss the hole so bright.
And though the little fellow tried and tried,
He couldn't get it right.

At last he sprawled upon the floor
With a sad and tear-lined face.
"Shoelaces is too hard to do,
They just doesn't want to lace."

A few days later a persistent child
Laced his shoes to the very top.
He beamed a smile at Mommy, and said,
"Things do, if you try and don't stop."

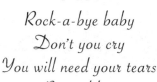

Rock-a-bye baby
Don't you cry
You will need your tears
By and by.

Little Dirty Faces

My, what a dirty little face
All smeared with mud, jam, and tears.
Dirty jeans and T-shirt, too,
You're sure a mess for your years.

But dirt and jam can be washed away,
And a child made sweet and clean,
All ready to play in the mud again
With no harm done in between.

Oh, face with innocence in its eyes,
Oh, child unsullied today,
Take care lest the soul become tarnished tomorrow
With dirt that will not wash away.

Mother keep a watchful eye,
Lest the fledglings
Come to grief
Unprepared to fly.

Children can make you confused.
You scold them 'til you're blue.
Then they look at you with innocent eyes,
That ask what is wrong with you.

A Matter of Opinion

Naive and innocent, a little child very often annoys
With his constant chatter and bumblings,
And his constant demand for toys.
He can stand in a dirty overall
With mud on his face and hands,
And tell you, "Me isn't doin' nothin',
Me is only playin' in sand."

Kids don't need to be just right,
Beneath the skies above.
All they require is patience,
And a large supply of love.

Teenage kids really like to roam
And do the teenage thing;
They only seem to remain indoors,
When there's work to do in spring.

The Resting Hour

The day had been a busy one
With endless things to do;
Washing clothes and window glass
And mountains of dishes, too.

Throughout the day my tiny son
Annoyed me with his din,
Asking questions, wanting time
'Til I was most done in.

At last, day's end, and Junior abed,
I settle down for inventory.
But no sooner do I sit when a voice says,
"Mommy, you've been restin'
Now will you tell me a 'tory?"

We often tire of childhood's questioning,
    So difficult to find a right reply;
And just as we're sure we have the answer,
Along comes the unanswerable query, "Why?"

All Bugs Take Care!

Caterpillar, watch your way,
For a little boy in blue
Has eyes upon your furry coat.
No telling what he'll do!

Mothers with small youngsters
Find very little rest.
They cannot know these are the years
They will remember best.

Boy of Four

Little innocence with grimy hands,
Beguiling, yet unaware,
The earth is your own, with its wiggle worms
and gay colored pebbles,
Exploring, absorbing, sans worry or care.

With open-eyed wonder and impish smile
You bounce your way along.
At times annoying, at times filled with mischief,
In your heart you conceive no wrong.

Grow you must, little freckle-faced lad—
Leave your baubles and pleasurable way.
May the cares of the world always rest on you
As lightly as they do today.

Junior stood in the doorway;
I'd just had a fall most annoying.
"You wouldn't fall," he said quite firmly,
"If you looked where you was going."

Youth

Hands in pockets, tousle-headed,
You go your leisured way.
Boy of eight, unscathed, unbroken,
Serenely accepting each fleeting day.

The world is your own in an open field,
Yours the sky and a babbling brook.
Time for play, for shouting and leaping,
Or sometimes the quiet of a secret nook.

Dream your dreams lad, play with glee,
Run in the wind with hair windblown.
In your innocent acceptance of all there is,
Your faith transcends my own.

Pa likes open windows;
Ma can't stand the drafts.
When the windows go up and down,
The kids can't hide the laughs.

The Windblown Lass

Checkered bonnet drooping down,
Blond tresses vexed by soft winds blowing,
Unruffled lass with cheeks aglow,
Half-hid by tall grass growing.

Naïve and vulnerable windblown miss,
In your bright pinafore—hair soft-curled—
Yet, in the promise of such as these,
Lies the hope of the world.

Daughter likes a certain boy,
You disagree, it's true.
But when a girl is seventeen,
There's nothing you can do.

I Want Mommy

Children can be most imminent,
When you cannot be there.
Knowing they demand attention,
Adds to your despair.

You've prepared a room for small ones,
With toys of every design,
Placed cookies about, and blown-up balloons,
To give them peace of mind.

Yet tears aplenty and saddened faces,
Come to your heart-filled view,
"Mommy, you have to come," they say,
"We haven't a thing to do."

A child of three came up to me,
And asked me for a song.
I played with him and read to him,
But fell asleep before he was gone.

I am very fond of cookies,
But I can't really boast.
For when the cookie tray is filled,
It's kids who get the most.

Graduation

Growing feet and endless learning
'Til reward of cap and gown.
Forward marching into destiny,
Youth carries on.

The cycle moves relentlessly
Tossed about by fate.
Another life, another hope,
Another world awaits.

When you are young with children by the hand
You don't seem circumspect.
When you are old, bent and grey,
You get respect.

If kiddies knew what parents know,
It would likely be a shock.
They'd be telling Mom and Dad
Be home by eight o'clock.

CHAPTER
7

It's a Living

Each day I scrub and wash
'Til I'm clean as I can be.
I'm not sure if I'm pushing work
As much as work is pushing me.

ECN

Mamma's Wisdom

Can I be a better wife?
Yes, I can!
Can I live a finer life?
Yes, I can!

When my little one cries at night,
Can I arise and make things right?
Yes, I can! Oh, yes, I can!

Can I toil from sun to sun,
Tired before the day is done,
And can I be a cheery one?
Yes, I can!

Can I believe when things go wrong,
And sing a happy, lilting song?
Yes, oh, yes, I can!

If our errors were recorded
And never the good we do,
We'd all be so downhearted,
The sky would never be blue.

Go Walkin'!

Are you feelin' a wee bit weary?
Life lost its charm and seems quite dreary?
Take a walk in the brisk, fresh air,
Feel the bonny breeze ruffle your hair,
Renew your spirit, lose your care—
Go walkin'!

Watch the birds as they flutter by,
Hear their cheerful, exuberant cry,
Note the solemn hills in celestial grace,
Let the cooling mist bathe your tired face.
Nature will caress you if you let her,
Now there, aren't you feelin' a whole lot better—
Out walkin'?

*When someone you care for
Has become out of touch,
You ponder the reason
You care so very much.*

Day by Day

Up in the morning, breakfast at seven,
Children to dress, beds made before eleven.
Dishes to wash and floors to make bright,
Vacuum the rugs and dust all in sight.
Clean the cupboards, bake a cake,
Dinner to think on—probably steak.
Put money by for the paper boy,
Grandchildren coming, look for a toy.

Don't forget the pizza for lunch,
And something to drink, such as soda or punch.
Fold the laundry, make ready to store,
Then put the clothes neatly away in a drawer.
Socks in the basket, ready to mend,
Ladies' meeting today, be sure to attend.
Bills to be noted and also paid,
Then off in a hurry to the Ladies' Aid.

Friends come to greet you and advise you to slow,
But the day is not over, while you're still on the go.
Dinner prepared and all gather round,
The day has been busy and most profound.
Father returns and we hear him say,
"What on earth have you been doing all day?"

Eating Time

Getting very close to lunch,
Not a bite since five.
My stomach growls; I'm a bit chafed;
Hope I can survive.

A cereal breakfast kept me agoin'
From early morn 'til two.
Then we ate from leftovers
To stop the gnawing chew.

I put the kettle on the stove
To have a cup of tea.
I forgot to put the heater on—
That's me.

When your man comes home from the job,
Quite sure you're not a winner,
Take him to an eating place,
Where you pay twenty bucks for dinner.

The Local Train

The trestle is gone from its 'customed place
Where the midnight special once echoed its call.
The whistled oo-a-oo broke the still of the night
Sending shivers of wanderlust through us all.

No clunking reverberance resounds on the steel rails,
No somber bell to clang and chime.
An era has passed into eternity,
A page has been written in the tomes of time.

It's hard to part with kids that marry,
Poor mother hits the skids.
Don't worry, Mom, they'll soon be back
With a houseful of noisy kids!

Daughter is coming to visit,
The eldest of our union.
We plan the meals and clean the place,
Though she only desires communion.

Priorities

We women are thought quite frivolous
In the ways that we spend, no doubt.
Often we purchase ridiculous things,
Which seemingly we could do without.

But while the needs of the day are constant,
And treasured joys are few,
Loveliness is an essential part
Of daily living, too.

Beauty is the antidote
That sweetens the daily mold;
Our everyday wants are transient,
But beauty refreshes the soul.

A one-time beauty came to visit;
I was filled with delight and glee,
To find she had changed throughout the years,
And looked a bit older than me!

The family of eight in the house next door
Decided to come to tea.
Ma put on her best store dress,
And left quite hurriedly.

The Weekly Wash

A housewife has her cleaning times
And a special day to wash.
Monday seems to be a favored time
For laundry day, "by gosh."

The Ladies' Aid may meet unattended,
And friends can go places galore,
But an honestly dedicated woman
Is reluctant to go to the store.

Windows, doors, and woodwork
Must wait for a distant sun,
For when mother has the washer going
Nothing else gets done.

She looked into her well-filled closet,
She wore a look of bleak despair,
Then turned to her waiting hubby and said,
"I haven't a thing to wear."

A Day Off

When he has unlimited time,
And wonders what to do next,
He spends a great deal of it
Feeling sort of vexed.

No desire for leisurely walking,
When there's no one for company.
He could mow the lawn, two inches high,
But it's not his cup of tea.

The spouse needs help with daily chores,
Though that would not be fun.
After sitting around with nothing to do,
He finds his day is done.

When the latest scandal is on TV,
It doesn't help the spirit,
But one must listen extra good
To be quite sure we hear it.

Men want a proper partner,
Who makes them feel quite wise.
But women are a bit astute,
And like it otherwise.

Pondering

When it rains or
When I'm indoors for a day,
I sit and remember
Times more gay.

Trips in the car,
Children's recitals,
And arms about you,
Warming the vitals.

Poems and essays,
And the golden rule,
And the cards that told us
They did well in school.

Remembering little kindnesses
When events were a bit sad,
Tokens of love
For Mom and Dad.

All is not forgotten,
Though we are apart,
Nothing is lost in time;
It remains within the heart.

Holidays

Holidays come upon us
A time for recreation.
A time to visit here and there
To travel all over creation.

"Have a great day!" your friends will say
As you pack your new-bought clothes,
And you seem to hear it frequently
As you note each day that goes.

Then once again the time will come,
To call the end of it all.
And though you're tired right to your toes,
You really had a ball!

If I were lost and unhappy,
I'd shed a hundred tears.
If you were there to calm me down,
I'd smile a hundred years.

Day's End

End of day,
Beginning of gathering together.
Father returns from his daily work
Snow-covered from inclement weather.

"How was your day?" I hear Mother ask,
"Was it an endless round of tedious tasks?"
Uncomplaining, Father relaxes,
With the evening news and a preview of taxes.

Happy to be in his favorite chair,
And keeping an eye on young ones there,
He moves to turn the TV on
To keep up to date on news and song.

"Where shall we go?" Mom inquires with hope,
"To the movies or to the neighbor's for chess?"
Father rouses his weary bones,
No word of annoyance he says.

Though the look on his face shows plainly
A conflict he'd never win,
Wedded bliss is often promoted
By knowing when to give in.

Work

My daily work is sometimes a chore,
And I'd like to run away,
And spend my time at some form of
Pleasure or even play.

Heaven only knows I've earned my rest,
And can at last be free.
But sitting all day in an easy chair
Is just not my cup of tea.

I lost something I valued.
The situation couldn't be worse.
I finally found the miscreant;
T'was hidden in my purse!

Mom and Dad go on a trip
To get away from it all.
They are no sooner settled,
When they give the kids a call.

The Old Quartet

I can't forget the old quartet
That sang on the streets of our town.
Do Re Mi and La Ti Do,
Commenced their lilting song.

Their strains rang out on the evening air.
When the nighttime bells stopped ringing,
Folks gathered round to hear the sound
Of hometown boys a'singing.

Untitled

Bless us all for trying
To be what we ought to be.
We may miss by a mile,
But we can wear a smile,
Knowing we tried constantly.

8

Voices of Others

Yesterday I was feeling low,
Too steeped in myself to pray.
Then a friend came by to commiserate;
We're both doing fine today.

ℰCN

Old Friends Are the Best

I had a friend, a very good friend,
Who used to visit me.
But I moved one day to a distant place,
And we got out of touch, you see.

Then one day I opened the door
And there was my friend of old.
What a time we had together,
And the stories that we told.

Old photos we scanned—
We laughed and cried the while—
For each one brought memories rare
Of clothes now out of style.

We talked of sleigh rides and golden hours
And picnics full of fun.
Of the day Mother fell in the old frog pond
And had to dry her clothes in the sun.

Today we abound in numerous pleasures,
But the best of all to me,
Is to open the door and, when I least expect it,
Find an old friend come to tea.

The Weekly Bias

Each week when we ladies meet for bridge
And a friendly cup of tea,
The chatter often runs to gossip
Which comes quite naturally.

Ellen is not the woman she seems,
Joyce keeps a terrible house,
Old Jason cheats on his income tax,
And another cheats on his spouse.

Our ladies agree to snub the wayward,
On this point, not one will budge;
I'm not so sure that I can agree,
For who appointed me their judge?

Lock the door, pull the shades,
When a busybody comes around.
Whatever she sees, whatever you say,
Will soon be all over town.

Faces

Some folks' faces are a sort of facade,
Seeming outwardly harsh and anti-you.
Wouldn't it be nice to look inside
And learn what is really true?

Are you as inhospitable as you seem to be?
Or if I catch you quite unaware,
Will I perceive an angel lurking
With quiet mien and laurel in her hair?

But some folks cannot be analyzed
As to whether friend or foe;
'Twould be a nicer world, by far,
If one could really know.

A woman I thought reclusive
Came to visit me one day.
We visited over a cup of tea;
The occasion made my day.

A Matter of Years

An old man lives within our block,
He walks with crippled gait;
He carries a cane, and is sort of decrepit,
In a child's eyes a sorry estate.

I sat beside him on a bench
And spoke of games to play.
I told him if he'd follow me
We would have a super day.

The old man gently shook his head,
He said, "Boys like kites to fly;
I like to sit on a sunny bench
And with birds to sing me a lullaby,
Dream of days gone by."

Put the kettle on the fire;
Take dishes from the shelf.
If folks change their minds about a visit,
Sit down and feed yourself.

Gossip

When a neighbor came to visit
I'd rather she took a walk,
But I endured her conversation
For she knew the latest talk.

He wears his present status
As he used to wear a coat.
It covers up a lot of things,
He'd not want folks to note.

Faces from My Youth

In retrospection, I see the dear faces
Of the loved ones of my youth.
Their mannerisms and graces
No photograph could improve.
They harbored no intention
Of pride in their mode of dress.
They wore whatever was neat and tidy,
And let Heaven do the rest.

Folks who try for perfection,
Miss it by a mile.
They would likely be more accurate,
If they practiced how to smile.

A Master of Opinion

The women sat at the tea table,
In varying stages of vex,
Each voicing her disapproval
Of the late-coming Mrs. "X."

"She's far too preeminent, far too sure,
Too witty, too utterly gay."
Some said whenever she entered a room
Only she had something to say.

The latecomer bustled into the meeting,
Exuberant, friendly, without a care.
She seemed to me like a refreshing breeze
Sweeping in to clean up the air.

With a radiant smile she took her place;
She spoke of the lovely day.
Just being herself in a hostile room
(Unaware of rancor and shoddiness),
She serenely went her way.

If I were a queen of sorts,
I'd hold my head up high.
I think I'll do so, anyway,
When certain folks pass by.

A Disagreement

Folks sometimes assault you
With ideas not too true.
It's rather rude to disagree,
And present a different view.

So you stand like a soggy sponge,
Soaking up the waste;
Then you wish them happiness,
And leave the place in haste.

Some folks you like,
Some you don't.
I could be friendly anyway,
But I won't!

Don't find fault with a neighbor,
It's not the thing to do.
You would be far less confident,
If you knew what he thinks of you.

Lady of Gloom

A lady I knew in former days
Called me by phone to my amaze.
We talked for a while, I spoke of clime,
I inquired to learn if she was fine.

She complained most every minute,
Despising her abode and everything in it.
She spoke of the lands she had left with glee,
Expecting to be happy eternally.

Happiness is hard to find
It must be nurtured in the mind.

A Secret

I was told a secret,
I promised not to speak it,
But I told it anyway,
It was much too good to keep it.

To know the hurt of a slight remark,
Perhaps not intended to break you,
Also know that an angry return
May cause a loved one to forsake you.

The Golden Years

Squat, brown house in the valley,
Bathed in sunset's glow descending.
I peek and see Mother's grey-streaked head
Bent over the weekly mending.

CN

My Mother

White hair wisping in the wind,
Blue eyes ever aware,
Busily moving from place to place,
She seemed to be everywhere.

Work was her giving nature,
Gentleness shrouded her way.
Goodness beyond any measure,
Came natural to her as day.

Days end and a favorite chair,
Mother found a resting hour.
Is mending still upon her knee,
As she rests in a heavenly bower?

The household buzzes around you.
The day's work must progress.
In your former day, you longed for play,
Now you tire of rest.

Grandma

All day long my grandma sits
Before the television,
Watching family programs
'Til she's nearly lost her vision.

Susie's man has left his wife
And Laura's child is missing,
And Ellen wonders should John or Jim
Be the one she should be kissing.

And so it goes and Grandma cries
And avows she's never vexed,
And can't wait 'til tomorrow comes
To see what happens next.

*Folks still young and able
Think you are like they,
And can go about with nonchalance,
Come whatever may.*

Relaxation

When you were young
You waited for relaxation
And found it not amiss.
When you grow old and sit,
Very often,
You think, "How have I come to this?"

The old folks look back upon the years,
Oft with sorrow.
The young look upon today as the beginning
Of tomorrow.

You accept the hazards of daily living
For mistakes you can atone,
But nothing can lighten shadows
When you are alone.

Grandma's Apron

Grandma wears a calico apron
With a huge pocket she finds handy,
When little children are very good
She reaches in for peppermint candy.

Carpenters have aprons, too,
For such things as a wrench or a socket,
But no one has an apron like Grandma's,
For Grandma's heart is in the pocket.

Grandma's Day

Children scrubbed, and kitchen, too,
All is spruced up fine.
A delicious aroma fills the air
'Cause Grandma's comin' to dine.

Bring forth the finest china,
The teapot of gold design,
And lay down the lacy table cover—
for nothing's too good—
When Grandma comes to dine.

Days so special we will remember them,
Standing out in the realm of time.
Who can forget the joy and expectation
Of having Grandma come to dine.

Grandpa's Knee

Grandpa's knee is a bouncy place,
Loving, secure, and stout.
And Grandpa could tell such stories
As would make your eyes bug out.

Grandpa has gone where good folks go,
But he left a legacy;
For the ways of the wise and life's best lessons
Are oft learned at Grandpa's knee.

We were unaware of time passing by,
The children grew, we learned how years fly.
Always present, though miles apart,
Memory never deserts the heart.

Grandpa's Teacup

Every afternoon at three
Before the sun had waned,
Grandpa had a cup of tea
From an old cup, cracked and stained.

"This cup is mine," he oft observed
In no uncertain way,
"And if I hang it from a rusted nail,
Who has a thing to say?"

As years went by I became a man
With a little boy of three,
Who listened with solemn interest
To stories of Grandpa's special nail,
And his daily cup of tea.

We seniors must look presentable,
Like bookends on the shelves.
We may not have oodles of material things,
But we will always have ourselves.

Grandpa's Slippers

Each night when the evening sun went down
Grandpa would sit in his chair of brown,
And say, "Boy, you must hasten and upstairs go
And bring me my slippers with the hole in the toe."

Grandpa has gone and old days have passed;
The rose blooms and fades but the memory lasts.
I idly sit dreaming, and in reverie's glow,
Once more I see Grandpa and the old worn slippers
With the hole in the toe.

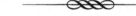

*A man who reached a hundred years
Spoke before a throng.
He said if he knew how long he'd live,
He would have felt youthful all along.*

*There are times in each and every life,
When one makes a mistake or two.
But regretting it all in the senior years,
Is an unrewarding thing to do.*

Seniority

These are the years of retrospection,
Days to reflect on activities passed.
No more to rush with strenuous striving,
For the things we once hoped to amass.

The passing of time alleviates yearning,
Makes undesirable what once was thought all.
No longer to pine for the great and important,
Finding abundance in the real and the small.

*The world is not a cage
For folks who feel no glow;
It's a garden filled with roses,
For those who make it so.*

*You didn't have the time, you say.
No reason, no real cause.
Funny thing, like everyone else,
You had what time there was.*

Destiny

We are the old—though they have named it differently.
By whatever titled spirit,
It is the same, the ultimate.

The end—or perhaps the beginning—
Who can divine?
Who knows what lies in the untried recesses of time?

Aged, they say; and the laboring,
Striving and desiring years all have merged
In eternity's endless song.

From the seed, the blossom, from thence to seed
The age-old order
Progresses on.

Yesterday and tomorrow now one with today
An entry in time's eternal log.
Our only hope, in destiny's harvest,
Our faith and trust in God.

Life is a rutted pathway
Filled with crevices and stones.
You travel with a belief in destiny,
And at times with an ache in your bones.

The Carver

An old man sits in the shafting light,
Be-spectacled, be-whiskered, and grey.
He holds a jackknife in his hand,
And he carves the livelong day.

A block of wood, long seasoned and dead,
Laboriously shaped and styled,
Comes to life as a work of art
Or a toy for a little child.

Skilled in labor, yet humble,
He seeks no greater prize
Than to know the delight of his handiwork,
And see joy in a grateful child's eyes.

It's foolish to regret the past.
If you had times of fun
Don't worry about it when you're old;
You can't change what you have done.

Sonnet to Getting Old

You're not young
When you no longer run
To fetch the news
When the mailman comes.

When places hurt
That have no reason,
When you are chilled
In the warmest season,

When the folks
You love so much
You seldom see,
And you feel out of touch.

It is a great day
When you find
You are not forgotten,
Or out of mind.

When I was in my forties,
Life was a constant spree.
I never knew 'til sixty-five
How great it is to be free.

Senility

Alone in our easy chairs,
We speak of days gone by.
Too old to be a part of things,
Too sensible to cry.

We find a sort of comfort
In each other's company.
A way of compensation
For whatever used to be.

For remembrance is the golden cord
That draws the whole together.
Sitting in our easy chairs,
Why worry about the weather?

Now that I have retired,
Having gone through storm and strife,
I find it difficult to realize
I'll be old for the rest of my life.

At eighty you look back on the years,
With a feeling somewhat blue.
What you seem to remember most,
Are the things you didn't do.

Being Old

Old is remembering the best of times,
It's singing the tunes we loved to sing,
Regardless of the rhymes.

It's enduring pain you had not known
before,
And forgetting acquaintances
Once known by the score.

It's clinging to memories once very dear,
And praying for the courage
To survive another year.

Only a photo to indicate,
The years of our sharing.
'Tis all that remains,
Of a lifetime of caring.

The Oneness of Time

Years of toil and troubled hours,
Little washable faces, with eyes ever asking;
Hurts to mend, kissing away teary showers;
No time to reflect, nor count time's passing.

The little figures have grown and gone.
Gone, too, are the jeans, so heavy with sand.
No small footsteps soil my floor;
No more to lift a caterpillar from a grimy, little hand.

Time for reflection is all I have left,
But memories, like sunshine, comfort the soul.
When I look upon a familiar scene,
I find, overall, a completed whole.

Old is looking behind you,
Remembering the love and the good,
Regretting mistakes, and happy to know,
You did what you thought you could.

A woman I knew accosted me,
I gave her a look sharp and cold.
All was fine 'til we conversed,
And she mentioned that I looked old.

CHAPTER
10

Sense and Nonsense

I can write nonsense

With proliference.

Even if it doesn't appeal to some folks,

It, yet, may make a difference.

ECN

End of the Line

Eighty years is a landmark—
An end as well as a start.
Not enough gumption to kick up one's heels.
No desire to follow the heart.

Life must continue its destined time,
And be accepted on its terms.
I must arise from my lethargy,
Go forth, and water my ferns.

There is a time to be very good,
A time to be a bit sassy,
But if I say what at times I would,
I'd be blown clean off my chassis.

I am not an expert
On the art of poetry.
I can only rhyme at times
To prove my literacy.

How You View It

My small T-shirted youngster,
Overly adventurous,
Climbed upon a kitchen chair
And broke my favorite dish.

In anger did I chastise him.
He seemed to be contrite.
And when I spanked him once or twice,
His face was a sorrowful sight.

I told him how remiss he was
To knock things from stool and shelf.
With a look of surprising disdain,
He said, "You isn't too hot yourself."

We were taught to sit down proper,
To be a kind of saint.
We found it quite impossible
To act like what we ain't.

A Big Deal

A small boy stood on a lonely bridge
As dejected as can be.
He poked between the rugged boards
Then fell to his hands and knees.

I asked him what was wrong,
That he seemed so sad and glum.
He looked up with tear-filled eyes, and said,
"I lost my bubble gum."

*Folks like to rush around
And make life a steady flurry.
Life goes on as usual.
Therefore, what's the hurry?*

Naturally

Traveling with children
Can be a trial.
It seems every mile along the road,
One or the other must leave for a while.

You try to be patient and understanding
And think of words most kind,
But sometimes you just can't help but wish
You had left the kids behind.

Obedience

Mamma is often strict with me,
I mustn't do this or that;
I mustn't tease my baby brother
Nor tantalize the cat.

I sort of listen, but I seldom mind.
Mothers scold a lot, and then
Don't seem to mind if you're not a saint,
And ease up a little now and again.

But Grandmas say just what they mean
And no fooling or you'll rue it.
When Grandma says, "You listen here,"
By golly, you better do it.

A Discussion

A group of old men sat about.
I couldn't hear what was being said,
But I gathered the topic was most intense
By the lift of a hand, a stomping foot,
And an occasional shake of the head.

Untitled

Yesterday has departed.
Tomorrow is a dream away.
If you have visions
Of grand decisions,
You had better ruffle your feathers today.

Folks have troubles from day to day;
No one escapes a few.
Telling one's woes to a friend who knows,
Relieves the pressure on you.

When a fellow speaks of marriage,
And his pals all laugh and scoff,
He wonders if he should proceed,
Or call the whole thing off.

Untitled

Happiness is something beyond our means or skill.
It comes upon us without our will.
If it were a substance we could grasp,
Or hold within our mind,
We could hold it tightly to the end of time.

Epilogue

This compilation of verse by the children of Elsie Nelson is a tribute to a great lady. Many of her poems were written by the light of a kerosene lamp, in quiet corners, stolen moments, or late at night when sleep was no escape from the cares of the day. Mainly they went unnoticed except for an occasional scrap of paper rolled up inside an old sugar bowl in the cupboard.

Through poetic messaging she wrote of matters big and small relative to the human experience. Hope and courage were common themes, and hardships she said were merely a base for better things. Perhaps this ideology fortified her will to survive the stress and strain of dreadful times.

No one can live in the past, nor would anyone want to relive the woebegone 1930's, but indelible historical markers make it impossible to forget. Her poem called "Resurrection" is a testimonial to the poverty and despair of the great depression and quite possibly when she discovered her own invincible soul. Life demanded much from her and she delivered.

Throughout her adult life she wrote poetry about family, human nature, and her rural environment. In her poem called "Lamplight" she wrote:

> *A mother is a lamp that lights the family,*
> *The glow that keeps all together,*
> *And when a good mother passes away*
> *That light goes out forever.*

Elsie Nelson passed away quietly on July 21, 1999 without cause for apology or regret. Her family readily admits that her lamp flickered, but to this day they proudly proclaim that the light from her lamp remains undimmed thanks to her poetry and the remarkable achievements of her children, grandchildren, and great-grandchildren.

Dorothy Sarasin

Wandering Verse
An American Keepsake

Elsie Nelson

Publisher: SDP Publishing

Also available in ebook format

Available at all major bookstores.

 SDP Publishing

www.SDPPublishing.com

Contact us at: info@SDPPublishing.com

CPSIA information can be obtained
at www.ICGtesting.com
Printed in the USA
BVOW06s0804261217
503668BV00010B/193/P